W9-AOZ-427

FACTS & RECORDS

SIMON & SCHUSTER BOOKS FOR YOUNG READERS
Simon & Schuster Building, Rockefeller Center
1230 Avenue of the Americas, New York, New York 10020
Copyright © 1992 by Grisewood & Dempsey Ltd.
First U.S. edition 1993
All rights reserved including the right of reproduction
in whole or in part in any form.
Originally published in Great Britain by Kingfisher Books, Grisewood & Dempsey Ltd.
SIMON & SCHUSTER BOOKS FOR YOUNG READERS
is a trademark of Simon & Schuster.
Series designer: Ben White Associates
Text contributors: Jill Bailey; Chris Maynard
Illustrations by: Diana Bowles / John Martin & Artists (pp. 47, 73);
Wayne Ford (pp. 34-5, 42-3); Chris Forsey (pp. 60-5, 70-1); Hayward Art
Group (pp. 4-11, 16-17, 22-33, 44-59, 66-9, 80-1); Maltings Partnership
(pp. 12-15, 18-21, 72-9, 82-8); Josephine Martin / Garden Studio (pp. 36-41).
Manufactured in Hong Kong

10 9 8 7 6 5 4 3 2 1   (pbk) 10 9 8 7 6 5 4 3 2 1

Library of Congress Cataloging-in-Publication Data
Pennycook, Veronica. Facts and records / by Veronica Pennycook.
p.   cm. — (Simon & Schuster picture pocket) Includes index.
Summary: Presents a variety of remarkable facts and records in
such areas as the natural world, the human body, and history.
1. Curiosities and wonders — Juvenile literature.   2. World records — Juvenile
literature.   [1. Curiosities and wonders.   2. World records.]
I. Title.   II. Series.   AG243.B26   1993   031.02 — dc20   92-19026   CIP
ISBN: 0-671-79149-4   ISBN: 0-671-79151-6 (pbk)

FACTS & RECORDS

VERONICA PENNYCOOK

SIMON & SCHUSTER BOOKS FOR YOUNG READERS
Published by Simon & Schuster
New York   London   Toronto   Sydney   Tokyo   Singapore

CONTENTS

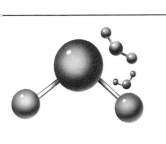

THE UNIVERSE

Everything that is in space makes up the universe. There is no end to the universe, and it's always changing.

Astronomers think there are at least 200 quadrillion stars in the universe. The stars are grouped into large clusters called galaxies, and there are millions of galaxies. Our planet is in a galaxy called the Milky Way.

FACTS & RECORDS

• The Milky Way contains over 100 billion stars. Of these, 5776 can be seen from Earth without using a telescope.

• The nearest star to Earth is the sun.

• Our galaxy looks milky because it contains so many stars all shining together.

MEASURING SPACE

The distances between stars are so vast that we measure them in light-years – that is, the distance that light travels in one year.

THE MILKY WAY

In the main picture, the Milky Way is seen from the side and our sun is shown by a red cross. Seen from above, the Milky Way is a spiral.

LIFE OF A STAR

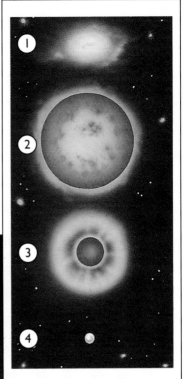

1 A star begins life as a cloud of dust and gas called a nebula.

2 The star begins to shine and becomes hotter and hotter until it forms a glowing red giant.

3 Gradually, the star runs out of fuel – it shrinks and its outer gas layers float off into space.

4 Over billions of years, the star cools to form a white dwarf and then it slowly fades away.

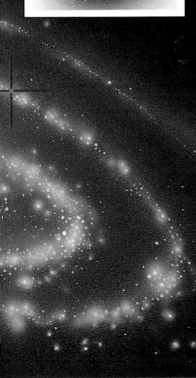

Our Solar System

Nine planets and their moons circle the sun to make up our solar system. Each planet follows its own orbit, or path, around the sun and is held in place by the force of gravity.

The Earth is just one of these planets. Over 4 billion years ago, the planets formed from the same huge cloud of dust and gas that formed the sun.

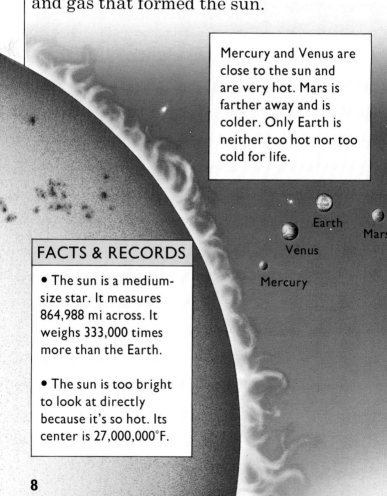

Mercury and Venus are close to the sun and are very hot. Mars is farther away and is colder. Only Earth is neither too hot nor too cold for life.

Earth

Mars

Venus

Mercury

FACTS & RECORDS

• The sun is a medium-size star. It measures 864,988 mi across. It weighs 333,000 times more than the Earth.

• The sun is too bright to look at directly because it's so hot. Its center is 27,000,000°F.

SOLAR SYSTEM FACT FILE

PLANET	DISTANCE FROM SUN IN MI	DIAMETER AT EQUATOR IN MI	TIME TAKEN FOR 1 ORBIT
Mercury	36 million	3031	88 days
Venus	67 million	7521	224 days
Earth	93 million	7927	365.25 days
Mars	142 million	4222	687 days
Jupiter	483 million	88,736	11.9 years
Saturn	887 million	74,568	29.5 years
Uranus	1783 million	32,313	84 years
Neptune	2794 million	30,076	164.8 years
Pluto	3666 million	1864	247.7 years

Jupiter

Saturn

Uranus

Neptune

Pluto

The five outer planets are very cold. Jupiter, Saturn, Uranus and Neptune are huge planets made up of swirling gas. Pluto, however, is even smaller than our moon.

WHAT IS A YEAR?

The Earth takes 365.25 days to orbit the sun. This is one Earth year. The farther a planet is from the sun, the longer its orbit takes and so the longer its year is.

The Moon

There are moons circling most of the planets in our solar system. Saturn has at least 18 moons, and even tiny Pluto has one small moon. The most familiar object in our night sky is our moon.

FACTS & RECORDS

• The moon measures 2160 mi across. It is 400 times smaller than the sun. But because the moon is 400 times closer to the Earth than the sun is, the sun and moon look about the same size to us.

• The Earth weighs about 81 times as much as the moon.

• It is always the same side of the moon that we see from Earth.

An astronaut on the moon sees the Earth in space, looking rather like a moon.

The moon's surface is covered with craters, plains and mountain ranges. The oldest rocks to have been brought back to Earth are 4720 million years old.

In just over 29 days the moon orbits the Earth, spinning as it goes. Unlike stars, moons and planets have no light of their own. We see our moon only because it reflects light from the sun.

SOLAR ECLIPSE

During its orbit the moon sometimes comes in between the Earth and sun. The moon can briefly blot out the sun, plunging the Earth into darkness. This is a solar eclipse.

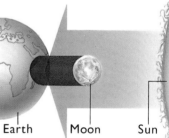

Earth   Moon   Sun

When astronauts explored the moon they had to carry a supply of oxygen to breathe because, unlike the Earth, the moon does not have any air.

Exploring Space

Rockets are used to launch astronauts and equipment into space. Equipment such as space probes and satellites orbiting the Earth send us back information. Ever since the first satellite was launched in 1957, we've been discovering more and more about space.

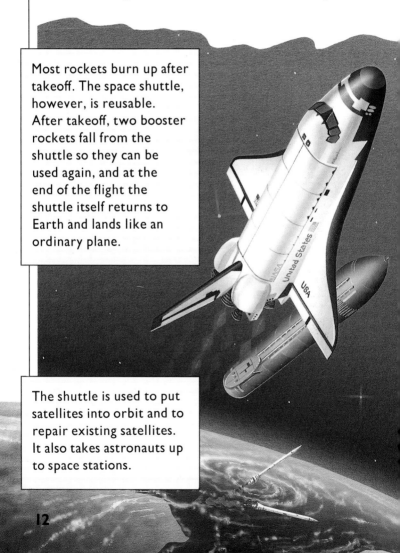

Most rockets burn up after takeoff. The space shuttle, however, is reusable. After takeoff, two booster rockets fall from the shuttle so they can be used again, and at the end of the flight the shuttle itself returns to Earth and lands like an ordinary plane.

The shuttle is used to put satellites into orbit and to repair existing satellites. It also takes astronauts up to space stations.

A FACT FILE OF FIRSTS

1957	Soviets launch the first satellite, *Sputnik 1*.
1961	Yuri Gagarin is first man in space.
1963	Valentina Tereshkova is first woman in space.
1966	Soviet space probe *Luna 9* lands on moon.
1969	Neil Armstrong & Edwin Aldrin land on moon.
1970	Soviet space probe *Venera 7* lands on Venus.
1971	American space probe *Mariner 10* goes into orbit around Mars and sends back information.
1973	Americans launch first manned space station, *Skylab*.
1974	Mariner 10 photographs Venus and Mercury.
1980	American space probe *Voyager 1* flies past Saturn.
1981	Americans launch the first space shuttle, *Columbia*.
1984	The first repairs are carried out in space, using the space shuttle to repair a satellite.
1986	American space probe *Voyager 2* photographs Uranus.
1990	*Voyager 2* photographs Neptune.

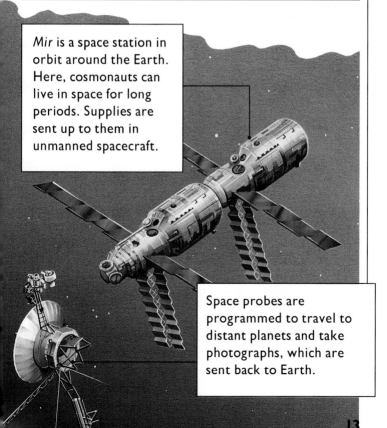

Mir is a space station in orbit around the Earth. Here, cosmonauts can live in space for long periods. Supplies are sent up to them in unmanned spacecraft.

Space probes are programmed to travel to distant planets and take photographs, which are sent back to Earth.

13

OUR PLANET

About 4600 million years ago, the Earth formed from a huge cloud of dust and gas. The Earth is made up of four layers – the inner core, the outer core, the mantle and the crust. It's so hot inside the Earth that parts of these layers are liquid.

The Earth's center is called the core. The outer part of the core is liquid and is about 1243 mi thick. The inner core is solid metal.

The inner core is 851 mi across and is as hot as 7232°F.

The mantle is about 1802 mi thick. It is so hot that some parts have melted into liquid rock and are constantly moving.

The crust is a hard outer layer that floats on the mantle. It is up to 25 mi thick under the land, but is only 4 mi thick under parts of the ocean.

Our planet is the only one we know of that has any kind of life forms. This is because it has the two vital ingredients for life – water and an atmosphere of oxygen. There has probably been some kind of life on Earth for 3.5 billion years.

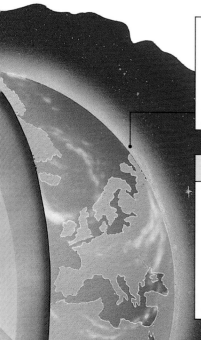

The Earth's atmosphere is a mixture of gases called air. Without the atmosphere, we would not be able to breathe.

MOVING PLATES

The Earth's crust is made up of about 20 pieces that fit together like a huge jigsaw puzzle. The pieces are called plates. As the rock in the mantle moves, the plates are moved too.

EARTH FACT FILE

Age:	About 4600 million years
Diameter (at equator):	7929 mi
Circumference (at equator):	24,902 mi
Total surface area:	196,949,842 sq mi
Land area:	57,258,630 sq mi
Water area:	139,690,980 sq mi
Average height of land:	2756 ft above sea level
Average depth of oceans:	12,451 ft below sea level

The Changing Earth

Over the years, many changes have happened to the Earth's surface because of plate movements in the crust. The plates are moved in different directions by currents in the mantle. Sometimes, two plates crash into each other, sending out shock waves that travel through rock as earthquakes. When plates are forced together, rock may be pushed up, making new mountains.

Melted rock from deep inside the Earth can well up through a weak spot between two plates, creating a volcano.

VOLCANO FACTS & RECORDS

- The world's largest active volcano is Mauna Loa, in Hawaii. It rises 13,675 feet above sea level. The lava from this volcano spreads out over 770 sq mi of the Earth's surface.

- When the volcano Krakatoa erupted in the East Indies in 1883, the sound was heard 3000 mi away in Australia! The island of Krakatoa was blasted into the air.

DRIFTING CONTINENTS

Over very long periods of time, the plates have moved the continents, or land masses, across the Earth's surface.

About 200 million years ago, all the continents lay joined together, forming one huge supercontinent. This split apart around 180 million years ago and the continents gradually drifted into the positions they're in today.

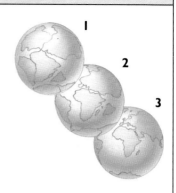

1 180 million years ago
2 65 million years ago
3 Today

EARTHQUAKE!

Over a million earthquakes happen every year, but only about 1000 are strong enough to cause damage.

When earthquakes take place under the sea, they sometimes cause giant waves called tsunamis.

HIGH MOUNTAINS

CONTINENT & MOUNTAIN	HEIGHT IN FEET
Asia	
Everest	29,082
Godwin Austen	28,252
Kanchenjunga	28,207
Makalu	27,823
Dhaulagiri	26,802
S. America	
Aconcagua	22,836
N. America	
McKinley	20,322
Africa	
Kilimanjaro	19,341
Europe	
Elbruz	18,482
Antarctica	
Vinson Massif	16,864
Oceania	
Jaja	16,500

Oceans and Rivers

Almost three-quarters of the Earth's surface is covered by water. There are four main oceans – the Arctic, Atlantic, Indian and Pacific – and many smaller seas. The largest ocean is the Pacific, which covers about 70 million square miles. Like the land surface, the ocean floor is constantly undergoing changes caused by plate movements.

Rain collects in ponds and lakes and flows back to the sea in rivers.

Most of the ocean floor is a vast, flat area called the abyssal plain.

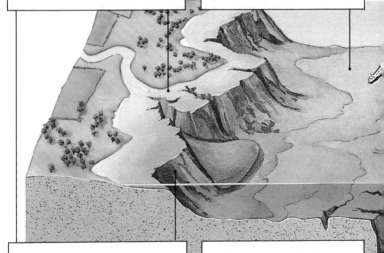

Around the coasts, the land slopes gently in the continental shelf, and then drops down steeply to the ocean floor.

Deep trenches in the ocean floor are sometimes made when one crustal plate is sliding underneath another.

LONGEST RIVERS FACT FILE

NAME	COUNTRY	LENGTH IN MILES
Nile	Africa	4160
Amazon	S. America	4002
Chang Jiang	China	3965
Mississippi-Missouri-Red	N. America	3710
Ob-Irtysh	Russia	3360
Huang He	China	2901
Zaire	Africa	2900
Amur	Asia	2744
Lena	Russia	2734

In places, submarine mountains rise above the surface to form islands.

Running through all the oceans are mountain ranges formed by lava welling up from beneath the ocean floor.

RIVERS

Rain and melted snow form rivers, which run toward the sea. Rivers sweep up stones that gradually wear away the rock they flow through, carving valleys.

As a river reaches the sea, it slows and deposits its load of mud and stones. This builds up flat mounds of land at the river mouth called deltas.

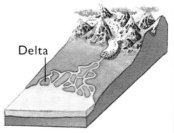

Delta

Weather

Weather is a mixture of temperature, wind, rain and sunshine. The sun is the main force behind weather. This is because the sun heats the Earth's atmosphere unevenly, creating huge masses of warm and cold air. The warm air rises and the cold air sinks – this movement causes the winds. The winds blow weather changes around the world.

Very strong winds cause storms. Tornadoes are fast, spiraling storms that happen in North America. They can sweep up animals, trees and people, dumping them far away.

HURRICANES

Hurricanes are tropical storms that are much bigger than tornadoes. A hurricane is usually about 186 mi wide. Its strong winds do a lot of damage and the rains they bring often cause flooding. The worst hurricane ever was in 1970 in Bangladesh, where floods drowned a million people.

FACTS & RECORDS

• The largest raindrop was .37 in across. It fell in Illinois in 1953.

• The heaviest hailstones fell in Bangladesh in 1986. They weighed over 2.2 lb each.

• The first umbrellas were used in China about 3000 years ago.

• The fastest flashes of lightning move at 86,996 mi/sec.

• The longest-lasting rainbow was in North Wales in 1979. It lasted over 3 hours.

• The most snow to fall in one year was 1224 in. It fell on Mt. Rainier, in Washington State.

• The most rain to fall in a month was 366 in. It fell at Cherrapunji, India, in July 1861.

• The driest place on Earth is Arica, Chile. It gets only about .03 in of rain in a year. The wettest place is Tutunendo, Colombia. It gets about 463 in of rain a year.

THE WATER CYCLE

As the sun heats the water on the Earth's surface, some of it turns into water vapor. This is a gas and it rises to form clouds. When the clouds become big and heavy, the water vapor drops as rain. The fallen rain collects in oceans, rivers and lakes, ready to go around the cycle again.

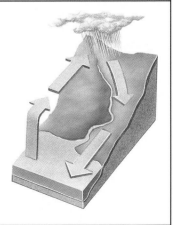

Climate

The climate of a region is the pattern of weather it has over a length of time. The world has six main climatic regions. The regions nearer to the equator are usually warmer climates and the regions at the poles are colder climates.

The eastern Sahara Desert in North Africa is one of the world's sunniest places. It has nearly 11 hours of sunshine each day – that's over 4000 hours of sunshine a year.

The coldest places in the world are near the poles – Antarctica, around the South Pole, and Greenland and Siberia, around the North Pole.

The Tropics are the most thundery region in the world. More than 3000 thunderstorms take place in the Tropics every night. This makes the Tropics the world's wettest region too.

WARMED BY THE SUN

The sun's heat is strongest near the equator where the sun is almost overhead. Since the Earth is round, the sun's rays have to spread out more when they reach the poles. This is why climates tend to be hotter near the equator and cooler at the poles.

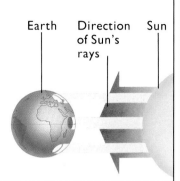

Earth   Direction   Sun
           of Sun's
           rays

CLIMATE KEY

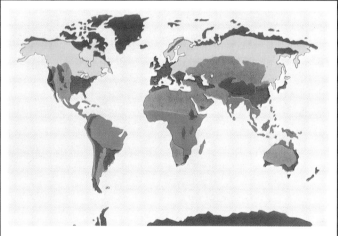

Polar – cold winter, cool summer. Very little rain or snow.

Cool & snowy – cool, snowy winter; hot summer.

Temperate – mild, wet winter; warm, dry summer.

Dry land & desert – very dry all year round.

Tropical – hot and wet throughout the year.

Mountain – climate changes with height above sea level.

COUNTRIES

Land covers over one quarter of the Earth's surface. We divide the land areas into seven continents: Europe, Asia, Africa, North America, South America, Oceania and Antarctica.

Continents contain different numbers of countries. At present, there are about 190 countries in the world, but this number changes from time to time.

EUROPE

Europe contains 42 independent countries. It covers an area of 4,053,278 sq mi. Its smallest country is Vatican City in Rome.

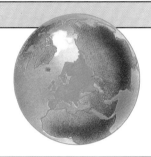

COUNTRY	AREA IN SQ MI	POPULATION	CAPITAL
Albania	11,100	3,250,000	Tirane
Andorra	188	52,000	Andorra
Austria	32,374	7,791,000	Vienna
Belarus	80,154	10,300,000	Minsk
Belgium	11,779	9,883,000	Brussels
Bosnia & Herzegovina	19,741	4,116,000	Sarajevo
Bulgaria	42,822	8,989,000	Sofia
Croatia	21,829	4,578,000	Zagreb
Czechoslovakia	49,365	15,283,095	Prague
Denmark	16,663	5,140,000	Copenhagen
Estonia	17,375	1,583,000	Tallinn

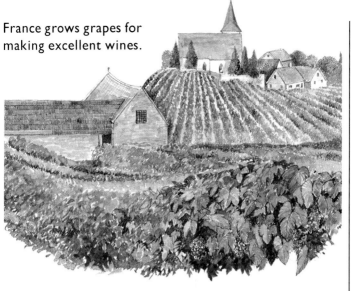

France grows grapes for making excellent wines.

COUNTRY	AREA IN SQ MI	POPULATION	CAPITAL
Finland	130,118	4,986,000	Helsinki
France	221,206	56,440,000	Paris
Germany	137,742	79,804,000	Berlin
Greece	51,146	10,269,000	Athens
Hungary	35,919	10,344,000	Budapest
Iceland	39,789	255,000	Reykjavik
Ireland, Rep. of	27,137	3,523,000	Dublin
Italy	116,302	57,690,000	Rome
Latvia	24,595	2,686,000	Riga
Liechtenstein	61	128,000	Vaduz
Lithuania	24,981	3,739,000	Vilnius
Luxembourg	998	384,000	Luxembourg City
Macedonia	9,928	1,914,000	Skopje
Malta	122	356,000	Valletta
Moldova	13,012	4,400,000	Kishinev
Monaco	.62	27,000	Monaco
Netherlands	15,770	15,019,000	Amsterdam
Norway	125,180	4,242,000	Oslo
Poland	120,726	38,180,000	Warsaw
Portugal	35,553	10,525,000	Lisbon
Romania	105,598	23,193,000	Bucharest

COUNTRY	AREA IN SQ MI	POPULATION	CAPITAL
Russia*	6,592,812	148,000,000	Moscow
San Marino	2	23,000	San Marino
Slovenia	7,819	1,884,000	Ljubljana
Spain	194,875	38,991,000	Madrid
Sweden	173,730	8,618,000	Stockholm
Switzerland	15,941	6,712,000	Bern
Ukraine	233,089	51,800,000	Kiev
United Kingdom	94,225	57,621,000	London
Vatican City State	.17	1,000	Vatican City
Yugoslavia	39,449	9,862,000	Belgrade

*Including the Asian part of Russia

ASIA

Asia has 48 independent countries. It is the world's largest continent, covering an area of 16,814,626 sq mi. China is the largest country in Asia.

COUNTRY	AREA IN SQ MI	POPULATION	CAPITAL
Afghanistan	251,772	16,433,000	Kabul
Armenia	11,506	3,300,000	Yerevan
Azerbaijan	33,436	7,100,000	Baku
Bahrain	258	503,000	Manama
Bangladesh	55,598	109,291,000	Dhaka
Bhutan	18,147	1,165,000	Thimphu
Brunei	2,226	249,000	Bandar Seri Begawan
Cambodia	69,898	6,701,000	Phnom Penh
China	7,566,369	1.16 billion	Beijing
Cyprus	3,571	707,000	Nicosia
Georgia	26,911	5,500,000	Tbilisi
India	1,266,588	843,931,000	Delhi

In Southeast Asia rice is grown on terraced hillsides.

COUNTRY	AREA IN SQ MI	POPULATION	CAPITAL
Indonesia	735,264	179,322,000	Jakarta
Iran	636,289	58,031,000	Teheran
Iraq	167,923	16,335,000	Baghdad
Israel	11,322	4,822,000	Jerusalem
Japan	145,855	123,537,000	Tokyo
Jordan	37,737	2,779,000	Amman
Kazakhstan	1,049,150	16,700,000	Alma-Ata
Korea, North	46,540	11,568,000	Pyongyang
Korea, South	38,025	43,302,000	Seoul
Kuwait	6,880	2,143,000	Al Kuwait
Kyrgyzstan	76,641	4,400,000	Bishkek
Laos	91,427	3,585,000	Vientiane
Lebanon	4,015	2,126,000	Beirut
Malaysia	127,748	17,861,000	Kuala Lumpur
Maldives	115	215,000	Male
Mongolia	604,243	2,070,000	Ulan Bator
Myanmar	261,787	38,541,000	Yangon
Nepal	56,136	18,916,000	Kathmandu
Oman	82,030	2,000,000	Muscat
Pakistan	310,401	112,049,000	Islamabad
Philippines	115,830	61,480,000	Manila
Qatar	4,247	422,000	Doha
Russia*	6,592,812	148,000,000	Moscow
Saudi Arabia	839,922	14,870,000	Riyadh
Singapore	224	3,003,000	Singapore City
Sri Lanka	25,332	16,993,000	Colombo
Syria	71,498	12,116,000	Damascus
Taiwan	13,885	20,454,000	Taipei

*Including the European part of Russia

COUNTRY	AREA IN SQ MI	POPULATION	CAPITAL
Tajikistan	55,251	5,300,000	Dushanbe
Thailand	198,455	57,196,000	Bangkok
Turkey	273,580	57,326,000	Ankara
Turkmenistan	188,455	3,600,000	Ashkhabad
United Arab Emirates	32,008	1,206,000	Abu Dhabi
Uzbekistan	172,741	20,300,000	Tashkent
Vietnam	128,400	66,200,000	Hanoi
Yemen, Republic of	203,849	11,282,000	San'a

AFRICA

Africa contains 52 independent countries. It measures 13,355,971 sq mi. Its largest country is the Sudan and its smallest country is the Seychelles.

COUNTRY	AREA IN SQ MI	POPULATION	CAPITAL
Algeria	918,492	22,971,000	Algiers
Angola	481,351	10,020,000	Luanda
Benin	43,483	4,736,000	Porto Novo
Botswana	231,803	1,291,000	Gaborone
Burkina Faso	105,869	9,001,000	Ouagadougou
Burundi	10,747	5,458,000	Bujumbura
Cameroon	185,567	11,540,000	Yaounde
Cape Verde	1,750	347,000	Praia
Central African Republic	240,533	2,740,000	Bangui
Chad	495,752	4,309,000	N'Djamena
Comoros	838	484,000	Moroni
Congo	132,046	1,843,000	Brazzaville
Djibouti	8,494	456,000	Djibouti

COUNTRY	AREA IN SQ MI	POPULATION	CAPITAL
Egypt	386,648	53,153,000	Cairo
Equatorial Guinea	10,832	348,000	Malabo
Ethiopia	471,773	50,974,000	Addis Ababa
Gabon	103,345	1,206,999	Libreville
Gambia	4,361	688,000	Banjul
Ghana	92,099	13,391,000	Accra
Guinea	94,971	5,071,000	Conakry
Guinea-Bissau	13,948	943,000	Bissau
Ivory Coast	124,502	9,300,000	Abidjan
Kenya	224,959	21,400,000	Nairobi
Lesotho	11,716	1,700,000	Maseru
Liberia	38,253	2,607,000	Monrovia
Libya	679,355	3,773,000	Tripoli
Madagascar	226,656	11,197,000	Antananarivo
Malawi	45,747	8,556,000	Lilongwe
Mali	478,764	8,156,000	Bamako
Mauritania	397,953	1,864,000	Nouakchott
Mauritius	790	1,075,000	Port Louis
Morocco	172,412	20,420,000	Rabat
Mozambique	309,482	15,326,000	Maputo
Namibia	318,259	1,874,000	Windhoek
Niger	489,189	7,250,000	Niamey
Nigeria	356,665	104,957,000	Lagos

East Africa's savanna lands are famous for the wild animals that roam there.

COUNTRY	AREA IN SQ MI	POPULATION	CAPITAL
Rwanda	10,169	7,181,000	Kigali
Sao Tome and Principe	372	16,000	Sao Tome
Senegal	75,750	7,113,000	Dakar
Seychelles	171	67,000	Victoria
Sierra Leone	27,699	3,516,000	Freetown
Somali Republic	246,299	7,114,000	Mogadishu
South Africa	472,356	23,386,000	Pretoria & Cape Town
Sudan	966,408	20,594,000	Khartoum
Swaziland	6,704	768,000	Mbabane
Tanzania	364,884	25,635,000	Dodoma
Togo	21,622	3,296,000	Lome
Tunisia	63,170	7,910,000	Tunis
Uganda	93,353	16,583,000	Kampala
Zaire	905,405	35,562,000	Kinshasha
Zambia	290,584	7,818,000	Lusaka
Zimbabwe	150,803	9,369,000	Harare

NORTH & CENTRAL AMERICA

North America has 23 independent countries. It covers 9,362,539 sq mi. The largest country is Canada and the smallest is St. Christopher & Nevis.

COUNTRY	AREA IN SQ MI	POPULATION	CAPITAL
Antigua and Barbuda	171	76,000	St. John's
Bahamas	5,380	253,000	Nassau
Barbados	166	255,000	Bridgetown
Belize	8,867	183,000	Belmopan

COUNTRY	AREA IN SQ MI	POPULATION	CAPITAL
Canada	3,851,768	26,219,000	Ottawa
Costa Rica	19,575	3,030,000	San Jose
Cuba	44,218	10,617,000	Havana
Dominica	290	81,000	Rosea
Dominican Republic	18,816	7,012,000	Santo Domingo
El Salvador	8,260	5,207,000	San Salvador
Grenada	133	97,000	St. George's
Guatemala	42,042	9,197,000	Guatemala
Haiti	10,714	5,486,000	Port-au-Prince
Honduras	43,277	5,105,000	Tegucigalpa
Jamaica	4,232	2,420,000	Kingston
Mexico	761,600	86,154,000	Mexico City
Nicaragua	50,193	3,871,000	Managua
Panama	29,208	2,466,000	Panama City
St. Christopher (St. Kitts) & Nevis	101	44,000	Basseterre
St. Lucia	238	148,000	Castries
St. Vincent & the Grenadines	150	113,000	Kingstown
Trinidad & Tobago	1,980	1,227,000	Port-of-Spain
United States	3,618,749	250,969,000	Washington D.C.

Nearly 8 out of 10 Americans live in towns and cities. The world's first skyscrapers were built in Chicago.

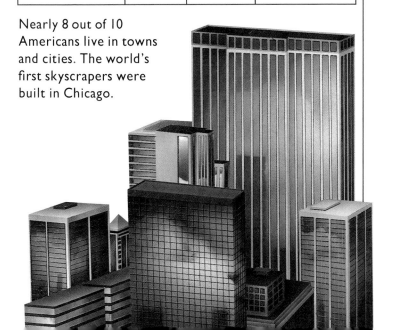

SOUTH AMERICA

South America has 12 independent countries. It measures 6,900,000 sq mi. Brazil is its largest country and Surinam is its smallest country.

COUNTRY	AREA IN SQ MI	POPULATION	CAPITAL
Argentina	1,065,183	32,322,000	Buenos Aires
Bolivia	424,163	7,400,000	La Paz
Brazil	3,286,451	153,322,000	Brasilia
Chile	292,255	13,386,000	Santiago
Colombia	439,732	32,987,000	Bogota
Ecuador	92,108	9,623,000	Quito
Guyana	83,000	790,000	Georgetown
Paraguay	157,046	4,277,000	Asuncion
Peru	493,220	22,332,000	Lima
Surinam	63,037	400,000	Paramaribo
Uruguay	68,037	3,094,000	Montevideo
Venezuela	352,141	18,105,000	Caracas

South America has a great variety of vegetation, from dense tropical rain forests to arid deserts.

OCEANIA

Oceania contains 13 independent countries. It covers 3,285,711 sq mi. Its largest country is Australia and its smallest country is Nauru.

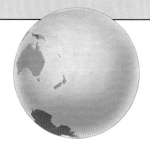

COUNTRY	AREA IN SQ MI	POPULATION	CAPITAL
Australia	2,966,183	7,086,000	Canberra
Federated States of Micronesia	271	107,000	Pohnpei
Fiji	7,056	727,000	Suva
Kiribati	266	72,000	Tarawa
Marshall Islands	70	48,000	Majuro
Nauru	8	7,250	Nauru
New Zealand	103,735	3,429,000	Wellington
Papua New Guinea	178,257	3,699,000	Port Moresby
Solomon Islands	10,640	299,000	Honiarar
Tonga	270	95,000	Nuku'alofa
Tuvalu	10	7,300	Funafuti
Vanuatu	5,700	147,000	Port Vila
Western Samoa	1,133	164,000	Apia

Australia has been an island for so long, it has plants and animals that aren't found in any other country.

33

THE NATURAL WORLD

Life first appeared on Earth as single cells. Cells are the building blocks from which all life forms are made. Over many centuries these early life forms evolved, or changed, and gradually separated into two clear groups – plants and animals.

A huge variety of life now lives on Earth, ranging from tiny bacteria to giant redwood trees.

There are five main groups of animals with backbones: fish (A), amphibians (B), reptiles (C), birds (D) and mammals (E). Some examples are shown here.

The main types of plants are seaweeds (1), mosses (2), ferns (3), grasses (4), flowers (5) and trees (6).

PLANT OR ANIMAL?

One of the greatest differences between plants and animals is how they get their food. Animals catch and eat their food, moving around so that they can do so. Plants, on the other hand, stay rooted in one place and make their food using sunlight.

THE IN BETWEENS

Not all living things are plants or animals. Fungi and bacteria are in between the two. They neither move around in search of food nor make food from sunlight. Instead, they feed on living plants and animals, or on their remains.

There are many more animals without backbones than with backbones. Spiders, flies, worms and snails are all animals that don't have backbones.

The Plant Kingdom

There are about 433,000 different kinds of plants – 285,000 are types of flowering plants and 148,000 are other types. Plants vary greatly in shape, color and size, and they can live in almost every part of the world. However, in order to survive, all plants need three things – sunlight, water and minerals.

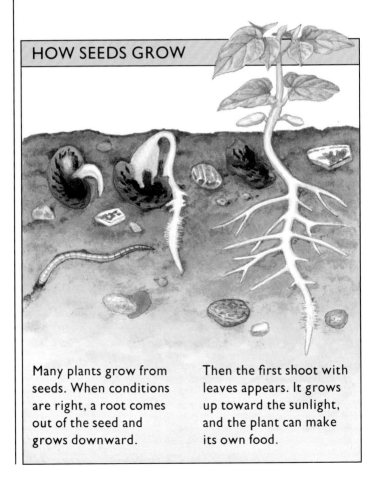

HOW SEEDS GROW

Many plants grow from seeds. When conditions are right, a root comes out of the seed and grows downward.

Then the first shoot with leaves appears. It grows up toward the sunlight, and the plant can make its own food.

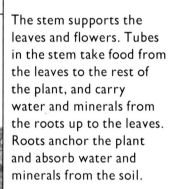

Seeds are produced in the flower. Leaves use sunlight to make food from the water in the soil and the carbon dioxide in the air.

The stem supports the leaves and flowers. Tubes in the stem take food from the leaves to the rest of the plant, and carry water and minerals from the roots up to the leaves. Roots anchor the plant and absorb water and minerals from the soil.

FACTS & RECORDS

- The oldest known living tree is a bristlecone pine that grows in California. It is 4600 years old.

- The Venus's-fly-trap is a very unusual plant – it eats insects!

- The largest and smelliest flower is the rafflesia in Southeast Asia – it measures nearly 40 inches across.

- Bamboo is the fastest-growing plant – it can grow 35 inches in one day.

The Animal Kingdom

There are between one and two million different kinds of animal alive today. Some animals, like the polar bear, live alone. Others, such as bees, wasps and ants, live in large groups that are highly organized.

But without plants there would be no animals on Earth, since all animals ultimately depend on plants.

A food chain is a way of linking up the animals that feed on each other. A zebra is a plant eater, and so it is the first animal in a food chain.

A lion comes next in this food chain since lions are meat eaters that feed on zebras. Most animals are in several food chains.

THE AGE OF INSECTS

Insects are probably the most successful animals on Earth. There are at least one million known kinds of insect and more are being discovered each year. All insects have a hard outer shell that supports their jointed limbs and most adult insects have wings.

FACTS & RECORDS

• The animal speed record on land is held by the cheetah, which can exceed 62 mi/h.

• The laziest mammal in the world is the three-toed sloth. It spends 16 hours out of 24 just sleeping.

• The ostrich is the giant of the bird world. It is up to 9 feet tall. Its egg can weigh 3.75 lb.

• The smelliest animal in the world is like a weasel. It's the African zorilla and it can be smelled from a distance of almost one mile.

• The common flea can jump over 130 times its own height.

• The world's largest locust swarm contained about 250 billion insects. It covered 2072 sq mi and weighed 558,800 tons.

• The blue whale's tongue weighs almost 4.5 tons.

• The smallest mammal in the world is Savi's pygmy shrew of Africa. It weighs less than 0.09 of an ounce.

• Some tortoises are thought to live for up to 200 years.

Animals on Land

Animals can be divided into two very basic types – those that have backbones (vertebrates) and those that don't (invertebrates). Many of the animals that live on land have backbones, including all the animals shown here. Examples of invertebrate land animals include many of the smaller animals such as spiders and snails.

Land animals have many different coverings. Cats and bears have fur to keep them warm. Tortoises have shells, which keep moisture in and enemies out. Elephants' tough hides protect them from enemies.

Some animals have coats that help to hide them from danger. A polar bear is white to blend in with snow and a grass snake is grass green.

LAND BABIES

Animals need to protect their young against enemies. Some snakes and lizards lay hard-shelled eggs in nests. Many small animals, such as mice, give birth hidden in underground burrows, where they can protect their young until they are ready to defend themselves.

WATER TO LAND

Marine turtles, seals and sea lions spend most of their lives at sea but lay their eggs or give birth on land. On the other hand, frogs, newts and salamanders live on land, but have to return to water to mate and lay their eggs, which hatch into tiny fishlike tadpoles.

FACTS & RECORDS

• The biggest land animal is the male African elephant – it stands 10 to 13 feet high at the shoulder. The average weight of one of these elephants is 6.25 tons.

• The biggest ape is the gentle gorilla. It can grow to 6 feet tall.

• The longest snake was a reticulated python from Malaysia, which measured 33 feet.

• The deadliest spider is probably the black widow of the Americas. Its poison is 15 times more powerful than that of a rattlesnake.

Animals in the Air and Sea

Insects, bats and birds are the only animals that can fly. A few other animals, such as flying fish and flying squirrels, can glide in the air but they cannot really fly.

A great variety of animals, ranging from microscopic creatures such as plankton to the largest animal – the blue whale – live in the sea.

FACTS & RECORDS

• A blue whale weighs up to 148 tons. It is the biggest animal that has ever lived, but it feeds on tiny plankton.

• The most poisonous jellyfish is the Australian sea wasp.

• The biggest fish is the whale shark. It can be up to 49 feet long.

Clams, octopuses and squid are mollusks. The largest is the giant squid – it can be over 60 feet long. A clam may live for over 220 years.

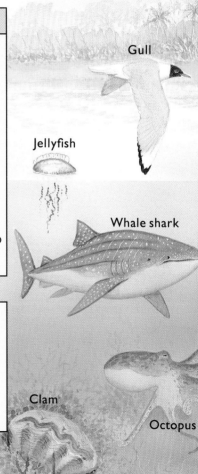

Gull

Jellyfish

Whale shark

Clam

Octopus

Birds fly by flapping their wings up and down and by gliding on outstretched wings. Bats flap wings made of leathery skin.

Albatross

Swift

Dragonflies

Butterflies

Hummingbird

The fastest flying insect is the Australian dragonfly, which can fly up to 36 mi/h. The monarch butterfly flies over 1864 mi in a year.

FACTS & RECORDS

• Hummingbirds beat their wings up to 80 times a second to hover while they feed.

• Swifts can spend weeks in the air, even sleeping on the wing.

• The wingspan of the wandering albatross can be 11.5 feet – longer than any other bird.

Fish swim by tightening the muscles along each side of their body in turn. They use their tail and fins to push against the water.

THE HUMAN BODY

You can't see it and, mostly, you can't hear it. But, day and night, there is a great deal happening in your body.

Every minute, your heart pumps 2.6 quarts of blood along a maze of arteries, veins and blood vessels. Laid out, these would stretch more than twice around the world. They carry blood to your 639 muscles to give them oxygen and food.

FACTS & RECORDS

• Muscles make up about 30–40% of the weight of your body.

• Joints let the bones move. Different types of joints allow the bones to swing around in many different directions.

• Blood is made up of red cells and white cells. Red ones carry oxygen. White ones fight any diseases and germs that invade our bodies.

• A sneeze is just a sudden explosion of air from the lungs. It can make air rocket from the nose at up to 103 mi/h!

PULL AND TUG

We have muscles so that our limbs can be moved. The muscles in the arm work in pairs. As one muscle contracts, or shortens, the other muscle relaxes. This causes the arm to straighten and bend.

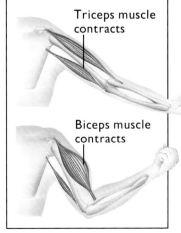

Triceps muscle contracts

Biceps muscle contracts

Adults have 206 bones in their bodies. The smallest bone is in the ear. It is only .1 in long.

The human skeleton is hard yet light because its bones have many air spaces within them.

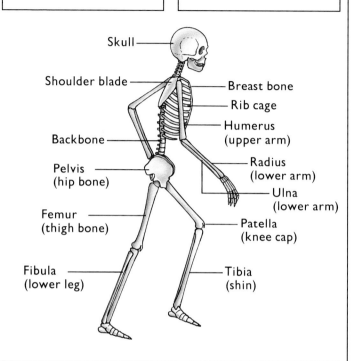

Skull

Shoulder blade

Breast bone

Rib cage

Humerus (upper arm)

Backbone

Radius (lower arm)

Pelvis (hip bone)

Ulna (lower arm)

Femur (thigh bone)

Patella (knee cap)

Fibula (lower leg)

Tibia (shin)

LIFE PUMP

The heart is a special kind of muscle that keeps the body supplied with oxygen. It beats 70 to 80 times a minute. One side of it pumps blood to the lungs, where the blood picks up fresh oxygen. The other side takes back this oxygen-rich blood and pumps it around the body.

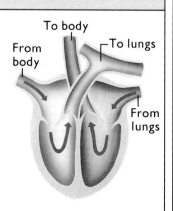

To body

From body

To lungs

From lungs

Our Senses

We have five senses – sight, hearing, smell, touch and taste. We use them to tell us about the world. If you grab a hot plate, touch tells you that you risk being burned. Sight and hearing help you to avoid bumping into things.

TONGUE TASTE TEST

Your tongue is covered with over 9000 tiny taste buds. Each bud has nerve cells that identify only one kind of taste – sweet, sour, bitter or salty. Different parts of the tongue recognize these different tastes.

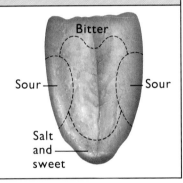

Bitter

Sour — — Sour

Salt and — sweet

FACTS & RECORDS

• Eyes move more than 100,000 times a day.

• Your body contains billions of nerve cells, carrying messages from all the parts of your body to the brain, and back again. Nerves work quickly. Some kinds can send 1000 signals per second to the brain, traveling at 200 mi/h.

• A complete layer of skin wears away and is replaced once every six weeks or so. The average adult has almost 2.5 square yards of skin.

• Nails grow at a rate of about 0.1 in a month.

• The human ear can tell apart more than 1500 different musical tones.

The millions of cells at the back of your nose can make sense of only 15 basic smells. But that's enough for your brain to be familiar with thousands of different kinds of smells.

Inside your eye, the lens throws light onto a part called the retina. From here, signals go to the brain. The lens forms upside-down pictures on the retina. The brain turns them right side up again.

Nerve endings in your skin feel heat, cold, touch and pain. Lips and fingertips are the most sensitive parts. They are packed with as many as 50 nerve endings per square inch.

Sounds entering the ear make the eardrum and the tiny bones of the inner ear vibrate. This sends signals to the brain, which then does its best to make sense out of all the noises it hears.

Food and Drink

During the course of your life you will eat about 55 tons of food and swallow approximately 44,000 quarts of liquid.

Inside your body, most of the food is broken down to provide the energy for movement. Some of it goes to making new body cells and repairing parts that wear out. Undigested food goes through you and out again.

THREE KINDS OF FOOD

All the different kinds of food that people eat belong to one of three main groups – proteins, carbohydrates and fats. Proteins help to build and repair our bodies.

Fats and carbohydrates give us the energy we need to stay warm and active.

Foods rich in carbo-hydrates

CALORIES

One way to find out how much energy we get from food is by measuring the number of calories in it. Rich foods, like oil and butter, have many more calories in them than things like pasta, bread and rice. Calories that are not used for energy can become fat.

Foods rich in proteins

Foods rich in fats

FACTS & RECORDS

• The biggest cheese ever to be seen weighed 40,000 lb. It was made in the U.S. in 1988 and was taken on a tour around the country in a special "cheesemobile."

• The most expensive food is black truffles, a kind of fungus.

• The oldest cake in the world was made around 2200 B.C. It was sealed and preserved in an Egyptian tomb.

• In China, a food delicacy is birds' nest soup – it's made from the nests of cave-dwelling swiftlets.

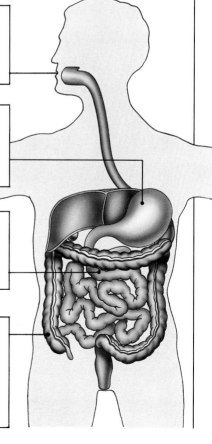

Food begins to break down as it is chewed and mixed with saliva.

Stomach juices digest it for about three hours and turn it into slush.

In the small intestine, the goodness in food is taken up by the body.

Undigested food goes into the large intestine, where water is taken out. The waste is passed out of the body.

Sports

Sports are games that have been enjoyed for thousands of years. Early hunters held competitions to practice their skills and to improve their fitness and speed. Today, many sports are organized events in which teams from different cities and countries compete vigorously against each other.

Some sports are based on the strength, or staying power, of an athlete. Swimming and running are two examples. Aside from clothes, participants don't need anything other than themselves. Other sports use simple equipment, like hurdles for jumping.

Many team sports need little more equipment than a bat and a ball. Yet it takes a lot of skill to play them well. Baseball, soccer, hockey, tennis and squash are played and enjoyed by people all over the world.

THE OLYMPICS

The first organized sports events were the Olympic Games, first held in Greece in 776 B.C. The modern Olympic Games began in 1896.

Olympics' symbol

Sports like cycling, skiing, motor racing and sailing all need to use amazing machines. The difference between winning and losing here may have as much to do with the quality of the machine as with the skill of its driver.

FACTS & RECORDS

• In 490 B.C., a Greek soldier ran from the battle of Marathon to the city of Athens with news of victory. Marathon races take their name from this event.

• The most famous bicycle race in the world is the Tour de France. It lasts almost a month and covers 2445 mi of French cities, plains and mountains.

• The biggest stadium in the world holds over 200,000 people. It is in Prague, the capital of Czechoslovakia.

• The first soccer World Cup was played in Uruguay in 1930.

• In 1924, the first winter Olympics were held in Chamonix, France.

• The fastest speed for serving a tennis ball was recorded by William Tilden in 1931. He slammed it at a speed of 163 mi/h!

ENTERTAINMENT

"All work and no play makes Jack a dull boy" is one way of saying that a life with no entertainment is horribly boring. But people have known this for ages – as the discovery of flutes and whistles that are 25,000 years old proves!

String instruments make music when their strings vibrate, by being plucked or played with a bow. Some, like electric guitars, have the sound boosted by microphones.

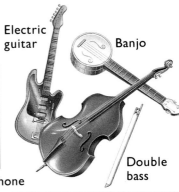

Electric guitar

Banjo

Double bass

French horn

Saxophone

Wind instruments are hollow and are played by blowing air into them. They may be made of brass, like trumpets, or wood, like clarinets.

Trumpet

Percussion instruments make sounds when they are hit or shaken. Although drums can play a few different notes, they are mostly used to play rhythms, or regular beats.

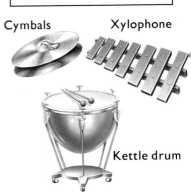

Cymbals

Xylophone

Kettle drum

MUSIC & DANCE

Every kind of dance has its own music. Flamenco is a Spanish folk dance that uses the music of guitars. Ballet comes from court dances in the 1600s. It is often danced to classical music. Disco relies heavily on electronic music and sounds.

Flamenco

Ballet

Disco

MUSIC FACTS & RECORDS

• The biggest-selling songwriter ever is Paul McCartney.

• The best-selling album of all time, with sales of more than 40 million copies, is Michael Jackson's *Thriller*.

• One of the greatest child performers was Wolfgang Amadeus Mozart. His first European tour was in 1762, when he was six.

• The first jazz record was made in 1917 by The Original Dixieland Jazz Band.

• The best-selling single ever was Bing Crosby's 1942 hit, *White Christmas*. It sold 170 million copies.

• The Beatles are thought to have sold over 1 billion records and tapes – that is more than any other pop group.

Theater, Movies and TV

Acting is a way of telling stories. The first theaters were in ancient Greece. In the Middle Ages traveling actors toured the land. In the 20th century, through movies and television, actors came to every town and, finally, to every home.

The Mousetrap is the longest-running play ever. It celebrated its 40th birthday in 1992.

Agatha Christie's
The Mousetrap

MOVIE FACTS & RECORDS

- The country that produces more feature films than any other every year, usually no fewer than 750 films, is India. In 1990 it produced 948 films!

- The most expensive film ever made was *Terminator 2*. The studio had very little change out of $125 million. It starred Arnold Schwarzenegger.

A FACT FILE OF FIRSTS

1887   Heinrich Hertz of Germany discovers radio waves.

1895   The first true motion picture is projected by Louis and Alphonse Lumière in France.

1897   German Ferdinand Braun invents the cathode ray tube, making television possible.

1901   Italian Guglielmo Marconi sends radio signals across the Atlantic.

1906   Canadian Reginald Fessenden, working in the U.S., succeeds in broadcasting speech and music.

Guglielmo Marconi

1910   Release of the first film to be made in Hollywood.

1920   The first radio station goes on the air in Pennsylvania.

1926   Scottish engineer John Logie Baird publicly demonstrates television.

Logie Baird's TV, 1926

1927   Showing of first film to include live speech, *The Jazz Singer* starring Al Jolson.

1928   Mickey Mouse appears in his first cartoon, *Steamboat Willie*.

1936   Regular television broadcasts in black and white transmitted in the United Kingdom by the BBC.

1938   First full-length color cartoon film, Walt Disney's *Snow White and the Seven Dwarfs*.

1940's radio

1947   The transistor is invented in the U.S. Small mobile radios using transistors are made from 1954 on.

1953   Color television is first broadcast in the U.S.

1956   Video recorder and tape are first demonstrated by American Alexander Poniatoff.

1985   Sony of Japan exhibits a television screen measuring over 1332 square feet.

1990   Over 2 billion people around the world watch the World Cup soccer finals live on TV.

Watching the World Cup, 1990

55

Books and Writers

More than 2000 years ago, writers such as Homer of Greece and Virgil of Rome produced great poems and plays that are still read to this day.

Novels, of the kind we read by the thousands in the modern world, did not appear until the 1700s. At about the same time, the first newspapers and magazines also began to be produced.

One of the greatest playwrights ever, William Shakespeare (1564–1616), wrote 36 plays and many famous poems.

BOOK FACTS & RECORDS

• The most popular book is the Bible. Over 2.5 billion copies have been printed – enough for half the people on Earth! The next most popular is *The Guinness Book of Records*.

• The longest encyclopedia ever created ran to 11,095 volumes. It was written by 2000 Chinese scholars in the years 1403–1408. The earliest encyclopedia was compiled c. 370 B.C.

A FACT FILE OF FIRSTS

Alpha | Beta

c. 3500 B.C. The Sumerians and Egyptians keep records by making picture symbols.

c. 1300 B.C. The first symbols of a Chinese script are written on bone.

c. 1000 B.C. The Greek alphabet develops. Its first two letters are alpha (A) and beta (B).

c. 700 B.C. The Etruscans of Italy adapt the Greek alphabet. This is later changed by the ancient Romans. Roman script is still used today when we write.

c. 500 B.C. Pens made from feathers (quills) begin to be used.

Quill pen, inkpot and script

A.D.700– 900 Printing with wooden blocks is developed in Korea and China.

c. 1050 Movable type first used in China.

c. 1450 Johannes Gutenberg uses a press to print the Bible at Mainz, Germany.

1565 First description of a lead pencil.

Early pencil

1798 Aloys Senefelder invents lithography. Images can now be printed from a flat stone coated with grease and ink.

1812 German printers Friedrich Konig and Friedrich Bauer use steam power to operate a mechanical printing press in England.

1884 The fountain pen is invented by Lewis Edson Waterman.

Gutenberg's press

1886 Ottmar Merganthaler produces the linotype machine that casts lines of metal type automatically.

1938 Ladislao Biro patents the ball-point pen.

1939 A photographic process is used to set type by W. Huebner in the U.S.

1980s Development of "desk-top publishing." Home computers can be used to create text and design and can print to a high standard.

Computer

Art and Architecture

Cave paintings show that prehistoric people liked to draw. Painting, sculpting and decorating pottery are other ways in which people have created beautiful objects. Even architecture (designing buildings) has become a form of art.

FACTS & RECORDS

• Probably the most famous painting in the world is the *Mona Lisa* by Leonardo da Vinci (1452–1519).

• In 1974, an army of 8000 ancient clay statues, all of them life-size, was discovered carefully buried at a site in northern China.

• The most expensive painting ever is Van Gogh's *Portrait of Dr. Gachet*. It was sold in 1990 for $82.5 million.

Cave paintings that are more than 20,000 years old have been found in a cave at Lascaux, France.

The Mona Lisa

MASTERPIECES OF ARCHITECTURE

The Eiffel Tower in Paris was built to celebrate the Paris Exhibition of 1889.

The Taj Mahal, India, looks like a palace, but it's a tomb. It took 20,000 men 18 years to build it.

The Great Wall of China was built to defend the border. It is 2145 mi long and can be seen from the moon!

The Sydney Opera House, in Australia, looks like a ship in full sail.

Taj Mahal

Eiffel Tower

Sydney Opera House

Great Wall of China

ARCHITECTURE FACTS & RECORDS

• The tallest building in the world is the Sears Tower in Chicago. It is 1462 feet tall.

• The Sultan of Brunei lives in the biggest palace on Earth. It has 1800 rooms and 260 bathrooms.

• West Edmonton Mall in Canada is the biggest shopping mall ever built. It has 840 shops in all.

• Of the seven wonders of the ancient world, only one still survives today: the Pyramid of Giza, in Egypt.

HISTORY

Although human beings have been around for several million years, our history begins only 5000 to 6000 years ago. This is the time when people first began to write things down. We divide history into three periods – ancient history, the Middle Ages and modern times. Modern history is the period from the 15th century to the present day.

MODERN WORLD HISTORY DATES

1453	Ottoman Turks capture Constantinople, ending Byzantine Empire. This date is taken as the end of the Middle Ages.
1492	Christopher Columbus discovers West Indies.
1493	Height of Inca Empire in Peru.
1516	African slave traffic to the Americas begins.
1517	German monk Martin Luther starts a movement to reform the Church called the Reformation.
1519–1521	Spaniard Hernán Cortés conquers Mexico.
1532	The Spanish under Francisco Pizarro conquer the Incas of Peru.
1534	Act of Supremacy: Henry VIII of England breaks away from the Church in Rome and makes himself head of the Church of England.
1588	Spanish Armada sets sail to invade England; defeated by English fleet.

Inca Empire

Martin Luther

1618–1648	Thirty Years War in Europe begins with Protestant revolt in Prague; ends with Peace of Westphalia.
1620	The first group of pilgrims sails to America.
1626	Dutch pilgrims found colony of New Amsterdam (New York).
1638	Japanese massacre Christians and stop foreign visitors to country.
1642–1646	Civil War in England: Parliament revolts against Charles I.
1643	Manchu dynasty founded in China.
1648	A second Civil War in England is crushed by parliamentary forces.
1652	Dutch found the first European settlement in South Africa.
1660	Charles II is restored to the thrones of England and Scotland.
1666	London is destroyed by fire.
1668	Spain recognizes Portuguese independence.
1688–1689	Glorious Revolution in England: Roman Catholic James II is deposed.
1689	France declares war on Spain and England.
1700–1721	Great Northern War: Sweden against other Baltic states.
1756–1763	Seven Years War: Britain, Hanover and Prussia against Austria, France, Russia and Sweden. Ends with Peace of Paris.
1757	Battle of Plassey establishes British rule in India.
1770	Boston massacre: British troops fire on American crowd, killing 5 people.
1773	Boston Tea Party: protest against tax on tea.

Spanish Armada

Pilgrim family

Fire of London

1775–1783	American War of Independence between Americans and British.
1776	American Declaration of Independence.
1783	Peace of Paris: Britain recognizes independence of United States.
1788	U.S. adopts its Constitution.
1789	George Washington is chosen as the first president of U.S.
1789–1799	French Revolution, starts with the storming of the Bastille prison.
1792	France is proclaimed a republic.
1792–1801	Wars of the First & Second Coalitions: Austria, Britain, the Netherlands, Prussia and Spain against France.
1796	Napoleon Bonaparte conquers most of Italy for France.
1798	Battle of the Nile: Napoleon's advance through Egypt is halted by British Admiral Nelson.
1801	Britain and Ireland are united.
1804	Napoleon is crowned Emperor of France.
1805–1808	War of the Third Coalition: Russia, Austria, Britain, Naples and Sweden against France and Spain.
1805	Battle of Trafalgar: Nelson defeats French and Spanish fleets.
1805	Battle of Austerlitz: Napoleon defeats Austrians and Russians.
1807	Britain abolishes slave trade.
1809–1825	Wars of Independence in Latin America.
1812	Napoleon invades Russia; he is forced to retreat, losing most of army.
1814	Napoleon abdicates; exiled to Elba.

Signing of the American Declaration of Independence

Storming of the Bastille

1815	Napoleon tries to regain power; finally defeated at the Battle of Waterloo.
1836	Great Trek: Dutch settlers (Boers) move north through South Africa.
1842	Britain defeats China in the Opium War and gains Hong Kong.
1846	Great famine in Ireland: a million people die, a million emigrate.
1848	Year of revolutions: in France, Berlin, Budapest, Milan, Naples, Prague, Rome, Venice and Vienna.
1854–1858	Crimean War: Turkey, Britain, France and Sardinia against Russia.
1861–1865	American Civil War over slavery; the southern states secede.
1863	Slavery is abolished in U.S.
1870–1871	Franco-Prussian War leads to the fall of Napoleon III, France is a republic again and Germany is united under William of Prussia.
1900	Boxer Rebellions against Europeans in China.
1905	Revolution in Russia leads to reforms.
1910	Union of South Africa is formed.
1912	China is declared a republic.
1914–1918	World War I: begun by assassination of Archduke Ferdinand of Austria at Sarajevo.
1916	Battles of Jutland and the Somme.
1917	U.S. enters war against Germany.
1917	Revolution in Russia: Bolsheviks under Lenin seize control.
1918	End of war as German offensive fails; Germany becomes republic.
1922	Russia becomes the Union of Soviet Socialist Republics.

Opium War

American Civil War

World War I

1929	Wall Street crash: start of world Depression.
1934	Hitler becomes führer of Germany.
1936–1939	Civil War in Spain: Franco becomes dictator.
1938–1939	Germany occupies Austria and Czechoslovakia.
1939	Russo-German treaty.
1939–1945	World War II: Germany invades Poland; Britain and France declare war on Germany.
1940	Germany invades Denmark, Norway, Belgium, the Netherlands and France.
1941	Germans invade Greece, Yugoslavia and Russia.
1941	Japanese attack on Pearl Harbor brings U.S. into war.
1943	Allies invade North Africa, Sicily and Italy; German army surrenders at Stalingrad in Russia.
1944	Allies land in Normandy, liberating France and Belgium; major Russian attack begins.
1945	Germany is overrun from east and west; Hitler commits suicide; atom bombs on Japan end war in East.
1949	Apartheid is established in South Africa.
1949	Communist rule set up in China.
1950–1953	Korean War: United Nations forces help defend South Korea.
1956	Soviet troops crush Hungarian uprising.
1961	Berlin Wall built.
1964	Escalation of American involvement in war with North Vietnam.

Lenin

World War II

Soviet troops, 1956

1967	Six-Day War: Israel defeats invading Arab armies.
1968	Soviet troops occupy Czechoslovakia.
1973	American troops leave Vietnam.
1973	The October War: Arab states attack Israel.
1973	Arab oil-producing states raise oil prices; leads to world economic crisis.
1975	South Vietnam surrenders to North Vietnam.
1975	King Juan Carlos restores monarchy to Spain after death of Franco.
1979	Vietnamese invade Cambodia.
1979	Shah of Iran is deposed; Ayatollah Khomeini sets up Islamic Republic.
1980–1988	Iran-Iraq War.
1986	Nuclear reactor disaster at Chernobyl, Ukraine.
1989	Chinese troops massacre student protesters in Beijing.
1989	Communist rule ends in Poland, Hungary, Czechoslovakia, Bulgaria, Romania and East Germany; the Berlin Wall comes down.
1990	East and West Germany reunite.
1990	Racial discrimination in public places in South Africa is made illegal.
1990	President Saddam Hussein of Iraq invades and annexes Kuwait.
1991	Gulf War: U.N. drives Iraqis out of Kuwait.
1991	U.S.S.R. is dissolved into its 15 republics.

Student protestors, Beijing

Berlin Wall comes down

Gulf War

Ancient Civilizations

Most ancient civilizations vanished after a while, which is why there are no Babylonians or Hittites walking around these days. There's one exception. China has an unbroken history as a great civilization that goes back over 5000 years.

Greek civilization began about 2000 B.C. The ancient Greeks were among the first people to have democratic governments, and their discoveries in science and math are used to this day.

In the 100s the Roman Empire reached from Britain to the Middle East – it was the biggest empire the world had ever seen. The Romans were great builders and engineers.

DISCOVERING THE PAST

Ancient civilizations are studied by archaeologists. They sift through the sites of early settlements, looking for evidence of the ways in which people used to live.

From the clues they find, such as pottery, coins and weapons, they piece together the jigsaw of what life must have been like many thousands of years ago.

The Egyptian Empire began 5000 years ago. It's best known for its huge pyramids, where the kings were buried with treasure. In 1922, Tutankhamun's tomb was discovered.

The ancient Chinese were an amazing civilization. They invented paper money, gunpowder, the compass and silk cloth. They had the world's first dictionary, and kept records of the stars.

Famous Explorers

One of the earliest stories of exploration is of a journey taken by a Phoenician called Hanno. In 480 B.C., he sailed from the Mediterranean to West Africa.

In 1271, 17-year-old Marco Polo went by land from Italy to a then mysterious place called China. Now that most of the Earth is known, the great explorers are the men and women who go into space.

In 1492, Christopher Columbus crossed the Atlantic and came across America. He'd set out for China and, to his dying day, thought he had landed in the Far East.

The South Pole was reached in 1911 by Roald Amundsen, just 2 years after Peary got to the North Pole.

THE *KON-TIKI* VOYAGE

Thor Heyerdahl sailed a raft across the Atlantic in 1970 to show how people once explored the world.

The first European to cross southern Africa was David Livingstone. In 1855 he reached Victoria Falls.

The first men to climb Mount Everest were Edmund Hillary and the Sherpa Tenzing Norgay in 1953.

EXPLORATION FACT FILE

DATE	PLACE DISCOVERED	EXPLORER
c.1000	N. America	Leif Ericsson (Norway)
1492	West Indies	Christopher Columbus (Spain)
1497	Newfoundland	John Cabot (England)
1498	Cape of Good Hope	Vasco da Gama (Portugal)
1500	Brazil	Pedro Alvares (Portugal)
1513	Pacific Ocean	Vasco Nuñez de Balboa (Spain)
1610	Hudson Bay	Henry Hudson (England)
1616	Cape Horn	Willem Schouten (Holland)
1642	New Zealand	Abel Tasman (Holland)
1728	Alaska	Vitus Bering (Denmark)
1820	Antarctica	Nathaniel Palmer (U.S.)

Famous Leaders

Now and again great leaders appear whose ideas and the example they set fill people with lots of enthusiasm. It may be an enthusiasm to wage war or to set themselves free, or to live peacefully and acquire great wealth.

Before the age of 33, Alexander the Great of Greece had conquered Egypt and the Middle East, and had reached Pakistan.

Genghis Khan and his Mongol armies created an empire stretching from China to the eastern edge of Europe.

356–323 BC

1162–1227

Napoleon conquered Italy, Spain, much of Europe and even reached Egypt. In 1804 he crowned himself Emperor of France.

Boadicea was the Queen of the Iceni. She led her tribe of ancient Britons against the Roman rulers of Britain. At first she had success, but she was defeated and died in A.D. 62.

PEACEFUL LEADERS

Mahatma Gandhi (below) led the fight for Indian independence from British rule. He was famous for getting his way by nonviolent means, and using public opinion.

1929–1968

Martin Luther King was an American pastor and civil rights leader. Like Gandhi, he believed nonviolence was the best way to highlight the plight of his people. In 1964, he won a Nobel Peace Prize for his work.

1869–1948

SCIENCE

Human beings have always wanted to know how things work. In the past, people often believed that the world was run by magic and heavenly powers. But today, we use science to explain things.

Science explores everything. It takes new ideas and uses experiments to test whether they are true or false.

BRANCHES OF SCIENCE FACT FILE

Astronomy	–	The study of everything in space
Botany	–	The study of plants
Chemistry	–	The study of what things are made of
Engineering	–	The science of building things
Geography	–	The science of the Earth's surface
Geology	–	The study of how the Earth is made
Mathematics	–	The science of numbers
Physics	–	The study of energy and matter
Technology	–	The use of science
Zoology	–	The study of animals

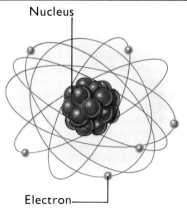

Nucleus

Electron

Everything in the universe is made of atoms. They are so tiny that even billions would take up less space than the next period. Most of an atom is its central part – the nucleus. Surrounding this is a thin cloud of tiny whirling electrons.

Steam

Water

Ice

SHAPE CHANGE

When a solid, like ice, changes to a liquid, like water, its molecules act differently. In solids, molecules are tightly packed. When a solid is melted, its molecules become loosely packed.

If water is boiled it becomes water vapor, which is a gas, and its molecules become even more loosely packed. That's the reason we can walk through clouds, swim through water and stand on ice.

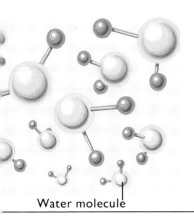
Water molecule

When different kinds of atoms are mixed together they form molecules. All the things around us, such as water, metals and plastics, are made of molecules. Molecules are the smallest part of something that it is possible to see.

73

Chemistry

Chemistry is the study of "elements" and "compounds." Elements are the basic materials from which all gases, liquids and solids are made. Elements mix together to create chemical compounds.

An element has only one kind of atom. Oxygen gas is an element. Salt, with two kinds of atoms – the elements sodium and chlorine – is a compound.

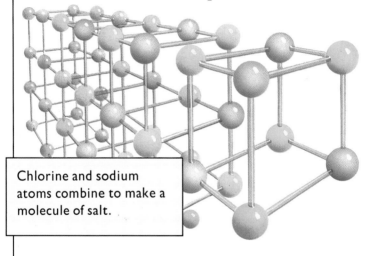

Chlorine and sodium atoms combine to make a molecule of salt.

COMMON CHEMICALS FACT FILE

COMMON NAME	CHEMICAL NAME
Baking soda	Sodium bicarbonate
Caustic soda	Sodium hydroxide
Chalk	Calcium carbonate
Hydrochloric acid	Hydrogen chloride
Lime	Calcium oxide
Plaster of Paris	Calcium sulphate
Table salt	Sodium chloride
Vinegar	Ethanoic acid

VANISHING ACT

When you stir sugar into a cup of hot tea it disappears. Yet the tea now tastes sweet, so the sugar is still there. It has dissolved – a chemical reaction has taken place.

BURNING

Combustion, or burning, is a very dramatic chemical reaction that happens when oxygen joins quickly with other elements. Flames, light and heat are given off.

In a wood fire, for example, the atoms in wood react rapidly with oxygen in the air. The wood gives out flames and it changes into ash.

FACTS & RECORDS

• About 4 million chemicals are known to science. They are being added to at a rate of more than 5000 new ones every week.

• The most common element in the universe is hydrogen. In the atmosphere it is nitrogen. In the Earth's crust it is oxygen.

• Over half the atoms in a person are hydrogen.

• When it's in the form of a diamond, carbon is the hardest element of all.

• The lightest element is the gas hydrogen.

• The lightest metal of all is called lithium. It weighs half as much as water.

Physics

Physics is the study of the building blocks of the universe – matter and energy. It looks at atoms and molecules, and the forces that hold them together. It also describes how light, heat and sound act on other things.

White light

Spectrum

Prism

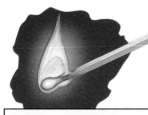

White light is a mixture of colors. A prism splits light into a spectrum that reveals each color. The colors of the spectrum are the same as the colors of a rainbow.

Heat is a form of energy. Heat can be created when an object is set on fire. It can also be created by the friction of two things being rubbed together.

Sound energy is formed when things vibrate. A hit drumskin shivers rapidly and makes the air vibrate too. When these waves of vibrations hit our ears we hear drum sounds.

Electric energy can be turned into other kinds of energy, such as heat (electric stoves) or light (light bulbs). It can also be stored in batteries to make flashlights work.

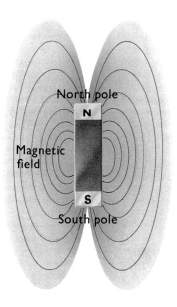

North pole

N

Magnetic
field

S

South pole

A magnet can attract
some other materials. It
has a north and a south
pole. Between these
poles are invisible force
lines known as a
magnetic field.

Every object that moves
has mechanical energy.
For a pendulum to
swing, it has to be
shoved. The mechanical
energy of the push passes
into the pendulum.

LIGHT EXERCISES

Light travels only in
straight lines. But it can
be bent in other
directions by a mirror.
Prove this by putting a
hand mirror at the edge
of a book or box. If you
peer into it you'll see
objects reflected in it that
are out of sight around
the corner.

Mirror

A coin that is invisible
from the angle shown in
an empty dish becomes
visible in water because
water bends light rays.

Empty dish

With water

Light rays
bending

Medicine

Medicine is the science of healing. On the one hand, it seeks to understand how the human body works. On the other, it examines what diseases do when they come into contact with the body. It also studies drugs and medical technology.

MEDICAL FIRSTS FACT FILE

BREAKTHROUGH	DATE	PIONEER
False teeth	700 B.C.	Etruscans
Microscope	1590	Janssen
Thermometer	1592	Galileo
Vaccination	1790s	Jenner
Stethoscope	1816	Laennec
Anaesthetic	1846	Morton
Antibiotics	1928	Fleming
Heart transplant	1967	Barnard

Bacteria

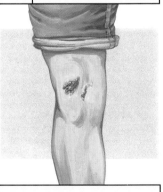

Diseases that make us ill are caused by tiny germs called bacteria. These can often be treated by antibiotic drugs.

The body has many ways of protecting itself. Small wounds grow scabs to keep out dirt and germs.

NEEDLE POWER

For over 5000 years, Chinese doctors have been sticking needles into people as a way to cure their ills. This is called acupuncture. The Chinese say the needles help to balance the body's energies and lead it to heal itself.

THE INSIDE STORY

There are many ways of looking inside the human body to check that everything is working properly.

X rays are used to reveal broken bones and diseased organs without opening up the body to look inside.

A stethoscope lets a doctor listen to your heartbeat and the sound of your breathing.

Tiny fiber-optic probes let surgeons go inside a patient's body with no more than a very small cut that can be covered by a Band-Aid.

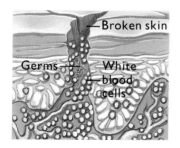

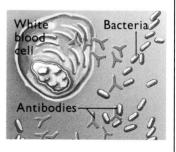

If a cut opens the skin, there is a second line of defense. White cells in the blood will attack any invading germs.

White blood cells make substances called antibodies. They attack invading germs and make them harmless.

79

Technology

Technology is the working of science in everyday life. Over the years, millions of inventions have made use of our scientific knowledge to improve our lives. We can produce heat and light, make cloth and steel, build televisions and computers, and even fly people around the world.

Steam-powered machines, like this weaving loom, could work much faster than the earlier hand-driven ones.

Computers can do many tasks faster than a person ever could. They can also be used to control machines automatically.

Powerful lasers produce thin beams of light that can cut steel or concrete very accurately. Other lasers are used for delicate surgical operations.

A HISTORY OF INVENTIONS

3200 B.C. Wheel – Mesopotamia.
3000 B.C. Glass – Egypt.
A.D. 950 Gunpowder – China.
1608   **Telescope** – Hans Lippershey.
1620   **Submarine** – Cornelius van Drebbel.
1698   **Steam pump** – Thomas Savery.
1712   **Steam engine** – Thomas Newcomen.
1767   **Spinning jenny** – James Hargreaves.
1785   **Power loom** – Edmund Cartwright.
1800   **Battery** – Alessandro Volta.
1816   **Camera** – Nicephore Niepce.
1839   **Bicycle** – Kirkpatrick Macmillan.
1845   **Sewing machine** – Elias Howe.
1849   **Safety pin** – Walter Hunt.
1852   **Elevator** – Elisha Otis.
1858   **Washing machine** – Hamilton Smith.
1866   **Dynamite** – Alfred Nobel.
1868   **Motorcycle** – Michaux brothers.
1872   **Typewriter** – Christopher Scholes.
1876   **Telephone** – Alexander Graham Bell.
1878   **Microphone** – David Hughes.
1892   **Vacuum flask** – James Dewar.
1892   **Diesel engine** – Rudolf Diesel.
1895   **Safety razor** – King C. Gillette.
1898   **Tape recorder** – Valdemar Poulson.
1901   **Vacuum cleaner** – Herbert Booth.
1924   **Frozen food process** – Clarence Birdseye.
1928   **Electric shaver** – Jacob Schick.
1930   **Jet engine** – Frank Whittle.
1935   **Nylon** – Wallace Carothers.
1945   **Electronic computer** – J. Presper Eckert & John W. Mauchly.
1947   **Polaroid camera** – Edwin Land.
1960   **Laser** – Theodore Maiman.
1961   **Silicon chip** – Texas Instruments.
1973   **Teletext** – BBC and ITA.
1981   **Space Shuttle** – NASA.

Early wheel

Tape recorder, c 1900

Early vacuum cleaner

1920s telephone

TRAVEL

Early travelers took many years to cross the continents and oceans. Travel was slow and dangerous. But modern transportation has made the world a much smaller place – a space shuttle can circle the planet at a speed of 17,275 mi/h.

In 1519, a seafarer named Ferdinand Magellan set sail from Spain with five tiny ships. One of these managed to sail 30,697 mi around the world. The voyage took three years and Magellan was killed on the trip.

A FACT FILE OF FIRSTS

1783	The first hot-air balloon flight is made in France.
1783	The first successful steamboat is built in France.
1839	The pedal-driven bicycle is invented in Scotland.
1852	The first powered airship is flown in France.
1863	The first underground railway opens in England.
1868	A steam-powered motorcycle is made in France.
1879	An electric train runs in Germany.
1885	The first gasoline-driven car is built in Germany.
1903	The first airplane flight takes place in the U.S.
1927	The first nonstop transatlantic solo flight, by Lindbergh.
1959	The hovercraft is invented in England.

In 1933, U.S. aviator Wiley Post made the first solo flight around the world in his plane *Winnie Mae* – it took 7 days, 18 hours and 49.5 minutes.

FACTS & RECORDS

• The fastest car speed is 633 mi/h, reached in a jet-engined car in 1983.

• The highest speed on water was 345 mi/h, achieved in a hydroplane in 1977.

• In 1976 a U.S. Lockheed SR-71A aircraft went faster than 2193 mi/h.

The first person to orbit the Earth was Soviet cosmonaut Yuri Gagarin. In 1961, his *Vostok I* spacecraft took only 108 minutes to make this historic flight.

Road Transportation

This is the age of the highway. In the U.S. alone there are over 3,479,840 mi of surfaced road, carrying more than 176 million vehicles. Yet for thousands of years before the car, carts and carriages were hauled by horses or oxen.

THE INTERNAL COMBUSTION ENGINE

Today's cars are powered by an internal combustion engine. Inside the engine, power is created by hundreds of mini-explosions that burn gasoline. Such engines were first built by a German, Gottlieb Daimler, in 1883.

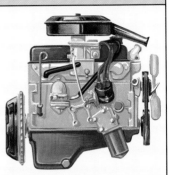

In the 1700s, passengers traveled by horse-drawn stagecoaches. Travel was slow.

From 1770 onward, road vehicles that made use of steam power were built.

THE MODEL-T FORD

The first motor cars were built by hand and were very expensive. In 1908, American Henry Ford decided to build cars more quickly by making them in a factory. Teams of workers assembled the cars on production lines. Cars like the Model-T Ford became affordable.

The Model-T Ford

This high-wheeled bicycle was built in 1870. It was nicknamed the "penny-farthing."

In 1885, German engineer Karl Benz built the first gasoline-driven car – it had only three wheels.

Rail and Air Transportation

The first public railroad opened in 1825 in northern England. Its engine, George Stephenson's *Locomotion*, could run at 15 mi/h. The railway age had begun.

In 1903, the Wright brothers made the world's first airplane flight. International airlines started in 1919.

The very first airship flew in 1852. In the 1920s, airships were built for international travel.

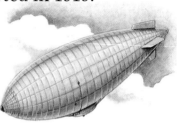

Unlike airships and balloons, the Wrights' airplane was heavier than air.

The 1923 autogyro was a plane with rotors. The first modern helicopter was built in 1936.

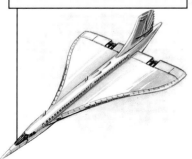

In 1969, *Concorde* became the first supersonic airliner. It can reach speeds of over 1305 mi/h.

FACTS & RECORDS

• The world's largest airport is in Saudi Arabia – it covers over 85 sq mi. The longest runway is at Edwards Air Force Base in California. It is over 6.8 mi long.

• The railroad built across the U.S. in the years 1863–69 was 1724 mi long. Today's longest railway is the Trans-Siberian – it runs 5865 mi from Moscow to the Pacific Ocean.

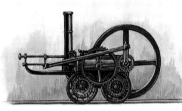

Richard Trevithick's 1804 steam locomotive was the first to run on track, in South Wales.

The fastest steam locomotive was the *Mallard*. In 1938, it reached 125.5 mi/h.

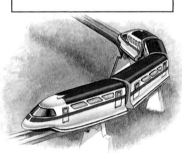

Monorails are trains that run on just one rail. The first monorail opened in Ireland in 1889.

The fastest railway train is the French TGV. In 1990 it reached a speed of 320 mi/h. It usually averages over 124 mi/h.

Sea Transportation

The very first boats were flat rafts made by lashing logs together with reeds. By 6000 years ago, people were building boats and had invented sails. Today, huge super-tankers are over 1600 feet long and weigh 605,000 tons.

FACTS & RECORDS

• It is thought that Aborigines used canoes to travel from New Guinea to Australia in about 55,000 B.C..

• *The Savannah* was a nuclear-powered cargo ship built in the U.S. in 1958. It could travel for three years without stopping for fuel.

• Modern Japanese cargo vessels have been fitted with computer-controlled sails so that they can cut down on fuel costs.

Outrigger canoes have sailed in the South Pacific for thousands of years and they are still used today.

Paddle steamers are driven through the water by paddles inside large wheels. Most now have just one wheel.

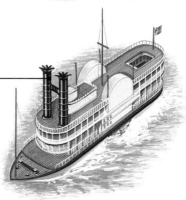

Clippers were fast, three-masted sailing vessels built from 1832 onward. They were used for trade.

The Queen Elizabeth II (QE2) is a luxury liner that was launched in 1967. It can carry over 2000 passengers.

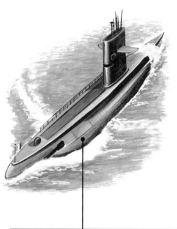

Hovercraft were first seen in 1959. They travel over water supported by a cushion of air.

People built all kinds of strange machines for undersea travel. The first modern submarine was designed in 1900.

FACTS & FIGURES

Which wedding anniversary does sugar stand for? How was it decided how long a mile ought to be? And where did the names of the days of the week come from? If these sorts of questions have ever stumped you, you'll find the answers on these two pages.

ANNIVERSARIES

1st	Paper
2nd	Cotton
3rd	Leather
4th	Fruit, flowers
5th	Wood
6th	Sugar, iron
7th	Wool, copper
8th	Bronze
9th	Pottery
10th	Tin, aluminum
11th	Steel
12th	Linen, silk
13th	Lace
14th	Ivory
15th	Crystal
20th	China
25th	Silver
30th	Pearl
35th	Coral
40th	Ruby
45th	Sapphire
50th	Golden
55th	Emerald
60th	Diamond
75th	Diamond

MEASUREMENTS

Ancient ways of measuring were often based on the body. The Egyptians used the span (the width of the hand) and the cubit (from fingertip to elbow) to measure the length of things. People still use the "foot" in the U.S. and other countries to this day.

A meter, however, is measured scientifically. It is measured in terms of the wavelength of light given off by an element called krypton 86. This is a rare gas found in the atmosphere. It has nothing whatsoever to do with Superman!

ORIGINS OF DAYS & MONTHS

DAY/MONTH	NAMED AFTER
Monday	The moon
Tuesday	Tiu, Norse god of war
Wednesday	Woden, chief of Anglo-Saxon gods
Thursday	Thor, Norse god of thunder
Friday	Frigg, a Norse goddess
Saturday	Saturn, Roman god of harvests
Sunday	The sun
January	Janus, Roman god of doors and gates
February	Februa, Roman god of purification
March	Mars, Roman god of war
April	Aperire, the Latin for "to open"
May	Maia, Roman goddess of spring
June	Juno, Roman goddess of marriage
July	Julius Caesar, a Roman general
August	Augustus, first emperor of Rome
September	Septem, the Latin for "seven"
October	Octo, the Latin for "eight"
November	Novem, the Latin for "nine"
December	Decem, the Latin for "ten"

TEMPERATURE SCALES

°Celsius		°Fahrenheit
100	Water boils	212
90		194
80		176
70		158
60		140
50		122
40		104
30		86
20		68
10		50
0	Water freezes	32
−10		14
−20		−4
−30		−22
−40		−40

HOW TIME IS MEASURED

1 microsecond	= 1000 nanoseconds
1 millisecond	= 1000 microseconds
1 second	= 1000 milliseconds
1 minute	= 60 seconds
1 hour	= 60 minutes
1 day	= 24 hours
1 week	= 7 days
1 year	= 52 weeks
1 year	= $365\frac{1}{4}$ days
1 decade	= 10 years
1 century	= 100 years
1 millennium	= 1000 years

INDEX